DRESS UP!

New fashion boutique design   Design de boutiques de mode
Diseño de tiendas de moda   Design de lojas de moda

promopress

DRESS UP!

New fashion boutique design
Design de boutiques de mode
Diseño de tiendas de moda
Design de lojas de moda

English preface revised by: Tom Corkett
French / Spanish / Brazilian Portuguese translation: Marie-Pierre Teuler /
Jesús de Cos Pinto / Élcio Carillo

Copyright © 2013 by Sandu Publishing Co., Ltd.
Copyright © 2013 English language edition by
Promopress for sale in Europe and America.

PROMOPRESS is a brand of:
Promotora de Prensa Internacional S.A.
C/ Ausiàs March, 124
08013 Barcelona, Spain
Phone: +34 93 245 14 64
Fax: +34 93 265 48 83
info@promopress.es
www.promopress.es
www.promopresseditions.com
Facebook & Twitter: Promopress Editions @PromopressEd

Sponsored by Design 360°
– Concept and Design Magazine

Edited and produced by
Sandu Publishing Co., Ltd.
Book design, concepts & art direction by
Sandu Publishing Co., Ltd.
sandu.publishing@gmail.com

Cover Images by All(zone)

ISBN 978-84-92810-94-9

Printed in China

CONTENTS

PREFACE

DRESS UP!

ASIA KORNACKI FROM PLAJER & FRANZ STUDIO

The role of stores has changed enormously in recent decades. No longer simply places that one enters with the mere intention of purchasing products, they have become venues for events, stages for exciting performances, and sometimes even new landmarks.

Fashion stores have been at the forefront of this shift. Some would even say that nowadays they are dressed up as much as their clientele! The transformation process seems to be an ongoing one that is shaped by current trends, shopping habits and technological developments in retail. Retail spaces have become statements that celebrate the brand and its products. They tell stories and communicate the philosophy, values and responsibilities of a company, as well as doubling as spots for happenings and events that bring like-minded people together.

Stores are "real" and "physical" places that create an engaging shopping experience. They bring a unique atmosphere into being and evoke emotions. Their design creates a world of its own and tells a story about and from this particular world. In this way stores offer multiple opportunities to engage with the brand and its values.

One of the greatest influences on the transformation of retail environments in recent years has been technology. The digital experience and the expansion of online retail have changed the entire shopping experience, including store design. A liaison of the virtual and the non-virtual plays a vital role and is becoming more prevalent in various store concepts, thus shaping the overall character and appearance of shops. Tablets and interactive screens or mirrors are now just as important in store design as display tables and shelves.

The very fast-paced fashion world, whose lifeblood is change and innovation, seems almost predestined to embrace new developments, whether of a technological, cultural or creative nature. Moreover, it is an extroverted world, one that shouts and screams, in some cases very loud, in others almost imperceptibly. The presentation of fashion collections starts as a show on the catwalk, continues as a created visual world on the pages of glossy fashion magazines, and ends up in stores, embedded in a retail design that creates the grand stage for them.

A range of these grand stages have been captured in *Dress Up!*, which offers ideas, solutions and different approaches to product presentation from all over the world, gathered on 240 colorful and inspiring pages.

Once the stories of these various trends and transformations are captured in a book like *Dress Up!* their place is written and sealed, meaning that on the one hand this book provides a wonderful source of information for the here and now, and on the other a formative retrospect for the future.

Enjoy your journey through this fascinating world and get inspired! And, of course, dress up!

PRÉFACE

DRESS UP!

ASIA KORNACKI, PLAJER & FRANZ STUDIO

Le rôle des boutiques et magasins a complètement changé au cours des dernières décennies. Ce ne sont plus des endroits où l'on va simplement acheter des produits : de nos jours, les magasins organisent des manifestations culturelles et des spectacles, et établissent parfois de nouvelles normes qui seront adoptées par d'autres.

Les boutiques de mode sont à l'origine de cette transformation. A l'heure actuelle, on peut dire qu'elles sont devenues aussi sophistiquées que leurs clients. Leur évolution constante est conditionnée par les tendances du moment, les habitudes de consommation et les développements technologiques du commerce de détail. Un magasin est aujourd'hui un espace qui met en scène une marque et ses produits. Il raconte une histoire et communique la philosophie, les valeurs et les responsabilités d'une entreprise. Il fonctionne aussi comme un lieu événementiel où se retrouvent les gens qui partagent la même vision des choses.

Un magasin est un espace physique réel aménagé de telle sorte que les clients se retrouvent dans un environnement agréable propice à l'achat. Il crée une ambiance et suggère des émotions. Son décor constitue un monde à part où tout tourne autour de cet univers hors du temps. Il propose aux clients de multiples possibilités d'interaction avec la marque et ses valeurs.

Le facteur qui a le plus contribué à la transformation du commerce de détail est sans aucun doute la technologie. Le numérique et le développement du commerce en ligne ont complètement bouleversé la façon de faire les courses et l'aménagement des magasins. Le lien entre la boutique en ligne et sa version non virtuelle s'est consolidé au point qu'il détermine la personnalité et le look des magasins. De nos jours, les tablettes, les écrans interactifs et les miroirs sont tout aussi importants dans une boutique que les étagères et les présentoirs.

Le monde de la mode en constante évolution est porté par le changement et l'innovation. Il est tout à fait logique que ce soit lui qui adopte en premier les nouveaux développements, qu'ils soient technologiques, culturels ou créatifs. La mode est un univers complètement extraverti qui s'exprime et se manifeste avec insistance ou légèreté suivant son humeur. La présentation d'une collection de mode commence par un défilé, continue avec des images sur papier glacé et se termine dans une boutique où elle est magnifiée par un décor conçu tout exprès pour la mettre en valeur.

Certaines de ces grandes « scènes » de la mode sont illustrées dans *Dress Up!* L'ouvrage expose différentes idées, solutions et approches de présentations de produits des quatre coins du monde. Ses 240 pages en couleur constituent une véritable source d'inspiration.

Dress Up! répertorie les tendances et les transformations du monde de la mode de façon à servir non seulement de source d'informations sur ce qui existe aujourd'hui, mais aussi de référence à l'avenir sur la situation de notre époque.

Bon voyage au pays de la mode ! J'espère que vous trouverez l'inspiration dans les pages qui suivent.

PREFACIO

DRESS UP!

ASIA KORNACKI FROM PLAJER & FRANZ STUDIO

El papel de las tiendas ha cambiado mucho en las últimas décadas. Ya no son aquellos simples lugares en los que entrábamos con la mera intención de comprar productos, sino que se han convertido en sedes de eventos, en escenarios de estimulantes actuaciones y hasta en nuevos enclaves emblemáticos.

Las tiendas de moda han encabezado este cambio. Incluso se podría decir que, en nuestros días, las tiendas de moda se visten y se arreglan tanto como su clientela. El proceso de transformación avanza impulsado por las tendencias más actuales, por los hábitos de compra y por los desarrollos tecnológicos. Los espacios de venta se han convertido en tarjetas de presentación de la marca y sus productos. Nos cuentan historias y comunican la filosofía, los valores y las responsabilidades de las empresas, además de ejercer como puntos de encuentro donde se realizan acciones y eventos que reúnen a personas de gustos similares.

Las tiendas son lugares reales y físicos que crean una atractiva experiencia de compra. Dan vida a una atmósfera singular y evocan emociones. Su diseño crea un mundo propio y cuenta una historia sobre y desde ese mismo mundo. De este modo, las tiendas nos ofrecen múltiples oportunidades para conectar con la marca y sus productos.

Uno de los factores que más han influido en la transformación de los entornos de venta en los últimos años es la tecnología. La experiencia digital y la expansión de la venta online han cambiado toda la experiencia de la compra, incluido el diseño de las tiendas. La relación entre lo virtual y lo no virtual tiene un papel clave; influye cada vez más en los diversos conceptos de tienda y configura el carácter general y la apariencia de los establecimientos. Las tablets y las pantallas o espejos interactivos son hoy tan importantes en el diseño de una tienda como los mostradores y las estanterías.

El frenético mundo de la moda, que se alimenta de cambio e innovación, parece casi predestinado a adoptar nuevos desarrollos tecnológicos, culturales y creativos. Además, se trata de un mundo extrovertido, que se expresa unas veces con potentes gritos y otras con voz suave. La presentación de colecciones de moda empieza como un espectáculo en la pasarela, se prolonga en un mundo visual creado en las páginas de papel *couché* de las revistas, y termina en las tiendas, dentro de un entorno que se convierte en su gran escenario.

En *Dress Up!* hemos reunido una selección de estos escenarios junto con ideas, soluciones y distintos enfoques de la presentación de productos en el ámbito internacional, todo ello recogido en 240 sugestivas páginas a todo color.

Las historias de estas tendencias y transformaciones quedan fijadas y encerradas en un libro como *Dress Up!* que, de este modo, nos ofrece una magnífica fuente de información sobre el presente al tiempo que un instructivo testimonio para el futuro.

Disfrute del viaje por este fascinante mundo e inspírese con las tiendas más *guapas* del planeta.

PREFÁCIO

DRESS UP!

ASIA KORNACKI, PLAJER & FRANZ STUDIO

O papel das lojas mudou muito nas últimas décadas. Elas já não são mais aqueles simples lugares em que nós entrávamos com a intenção única de comprar produtos, porém se transformaram em sedes de eventos, cenários de acontecimentos estimulantes e até mesmo em novos redutos emblemáticos.

As lojas de moda lideraram essa transformação. Poderíamos dizer, inclusive, que, na atualidade, as lojas de moda se vestem e se arrumam tanto como a sua clientela. O processo de transformação avança, impulsionado pelas tendências mais atuais, pelos hábitos de compra e pelo progresso tecnológico. Os espaços de venda converteram-se em cartões de visita da marca e dos seus produtos. Eles nos contam histórias e nos comunicam a filosofia, os valores e as responsabilidades das empresas, além de funcionarem como pontos de encontro em que se realizam atos e eventos que reúnem pessoas de gostos similares.

As lojas são lugares reais e físicos que criam uma atraente experiência de compra. Dão vida a uma atmosfera singular e despertam emoções. Seu design cria um mundo próprio e conta uma história sobre esse mundo e com a perspectiva desse mesmo mundo. Deste modo, as lojas oferecem múltiplas oportunidades para estabelecer a nossa conexão com marca e com os seus produtos.

Um dos fatores que mais influíram na transformação dos ambientes de venda nos últimos anos é a tecnologia. A experiência digital e o crescimento das vendas online mudaram toda a experiência da compra e, inclusive, o design das lojas. A relação entre o virtual e o não virtual desempenha um papel fundamental; influencia cada vez mais nos diversos conceitos de loja e configura o caráter geral e a aparência dos estabelecimentos. Os tablets e as telas ou espelhos interativos são hoje tão importantes no design de uma loja como as vitrines e estantes.

O frenético mundo da moda, que se alimenta de mudança e inovação, parece quase predestinado a incorporar as novas conquistas tecnológicas, culturais e criativas. Além disso, é um mundo extrovertido, que se expressa algumas vezes com potentes gritos e outras com voz suave. A apresentação de coleções de moda começa como um espetáculo na passarela, prolonga-se num mundo visual criado nas páginas de papel *couché* das revistas e termina nas lojas, dentro de um ambiente que se converte em seu grande cenário.

Em *Dress Up!*, reunimos uma seleção desses cenários, junto com ideias, soluções e diversos enfoques da apresentação de produtos em âmbito internacional, tudo isso em 240 sugestivas páginas coloridas.

As histórias destas tendências e transformações ficam recolhidas e gravadas num livro como *Dress Up!* que, desta maneira, oferece-nos uma magnífica fonte de informações sobre o presente e constitui, ao mesmo tempo, um testemunho instrutivo para o futuro.

Aproveite a viagem por este mundo fascinante e inspire-se com as lojas mais *elegantes* do planeta.

ACNE STORE IN TOKYO

ACNE

Swedish fashion house Acne opened their Tokyo, Japan store and the result looks great! Acne is a stylish Swedish fashion brand that's finally setting up shop in Tokyo, the brand is all about sleek and edgy Scandinavian ready-to-wear clothes. The name Acne stands for Ambition to Create Novel Expression, and the creative collective was formed back in 1996 in Stockholm, Sweden. Acne quickly rose to international fame with their raw denim jeans at the end of the last decade, and was one of the few avant-garde brands that brought skinny jeans back to the market.

The 260 meters of retail space, spread over three floors, will reflect the brand's image, as each shop is known as a studio, and aims to recreate the atmosphere of a creative working space. Running with the theme 'home within a store', the interior features wood, stone and fabric accents – fundamentally it appears Scandinavian yet channels the brand's edginess.

ACNE FLAGSHIP STORE NEW YORK

ACNE

ACNE FLAGSHIP STORE NEW YORK

ACNE

ACNE has designed a 4000 sqft flagship store at 33 Greene Street, Soho, inspired by its Stockholm base. The interior is bespoke to the NYC store and feature a floor framed by black and white striped tiles. A plush green carpet is sitting centrally in the tiles signifying the island of Stockholm, whilst the blue mirrored back wall symbolizes the water which encapsulates the Swedish capital.

The space division is set like partitions painted grey and framed in white, a reference to classic Swedish Gustavian design. The shoe salon to the back right of the store is lined in marble and features bespoke stools designed especially for the space. The ceiling is supported by hot pink and black steel pillars which punctuating the ceiling. It is a combination of three track spotlighting and bespoke LED lighting designed by ACNE.

PHOTOGRAPHY: ORESTIS LAMBROU
LOCATION: NICOSIA, CYPRUS

BLACK CELEBRATION CONCEPT STORE

PHANOS KYRIACOU

PHANOS KYRIACOU

On undertaking this project, the designer wanted to challenge the concept of the concept store by creating a versatile space able to accommodate several concepts at the same time. The space is visibly stripped down from all its initial fixtures (the flooring, the plasterboards, safety rails, etc.), whiles all the materials the designer brought in, are left pure and bear. The designer subsequently designed several autonomous project spaces, primarily by reinventing local elements. These spaces keep the shop in motion, by attracting different 'communities' of people (e.g. the book space, the music space, the clothes space). The main display of the shop(the music space), is a gigantic rendition of the traditional 80's multipurpose shelf called 'syntheto'; the dressing room is a copy of the designer's dad's office shed at his garage – he is a car engineer; the counter is an exaggerated version of a local desk design widely used in the 70's andthe80's. The lighting, a very important feature of the shop, is a meticulously designed light installation, which creates a balanced light flow in the space and activates the clothes' perform ability, illuminates their craft and accentuates the bareness of the shop.

The designer had to design every single element of the shop from doorknobs to clothes hangers, in order to fully realize his vision and successfully creating a self-contained universe. Coming from fine art/sculpture, the designer treated this project as an art project, doing what he know best, building an installation that invites the visitor to be curious, to discover.

PHANOS KYRIACOU

PHOTOGRAPHY: DIEPHOTODESIGNER.DE
LOCATION: SHANGHAI, CHINA

AEGIS FLAGSHIP STORE

COORDINATION ASIA

Aegis Shanghai is a premium men's boutique based in the heart of China, offering a unique selection of the very best contemporary designer and casual lux labels covering clothing, shoes, and accessories. With their brand concept and ideals in mind, COORDINATION ASIA aimed to create a space that highlights style, class and taste. Aegis' clientele is trend conscious, bold and expressive. The space needed to reflects this. The design concept originates from the classic library, with leather benches for ample seating and shelves to best display the collection. Natural materials such as wood and leather in combination with black glass create visual contrast, and represent a mixture of the classic with the new. The idea is that the modern man today doesn't simply runs blindly into the future; he respects and likes to hold on to his roots.

HOME /UNUSUAL STORE

LUIGI VALENTE STUDIO

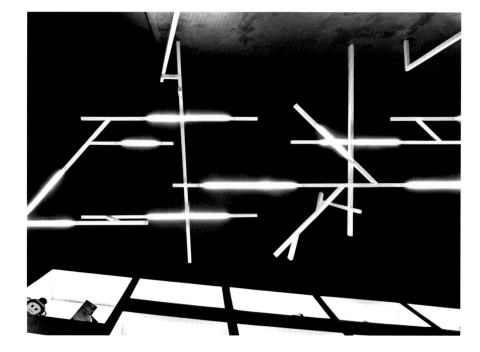

"Here is a song from the wrong side of town Where I'm bound to the ground by the loneliest sound and it pounds from within and is pinning me down" (Home - Depeche Mode). At the beginning, there was only the Depeche Mode song "Home". The store design was inspired by the dark style photos taken by Anton Corbijn who characterized the English group's graphics.

A place like home and, at the same time, a fantasy place that projects the client faraway. It is conceived as a display cabinet that uses pure elements in order to emphasize each cloth by creating a contrast with the steel structure. This structure both gives light to the main room and folds against the walls becoming a clothes hanger. The black color underlines the lighting system and creates a balance with the resins that cover both floor and left wall. Each element is used in order to emphasize the objects shown in it. This makes "Home" a unique store of its kind. The store plan is narrow and long; it gets even narrower in the back part. The client requested to keep the store wide in its central part. This allowed us to keep the restrooms at the end of the space, Advance from the dressing area / warehouse. The main idea was to create two different items exhibitors systems. On the right side, they follow a geometrical path: 18 plasterboards exhibiting niches have been created. They are lighted through neon lights covered by white plexiglass slabs.

In the lower part 6 big drawers have been created in order to be used as a storage space.

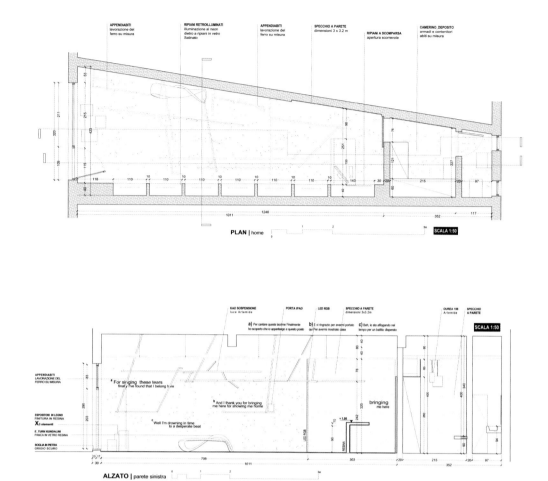

APPENDIABITI
lavorazione del
ferro su misura

RIPIANI RETROILLUMINATI
illuminazione al neon
dietro a ripiani in vetro
Satinato

APPENDIABITI
lavorazione del
ferro su misura

SPECCHIO A PARETE
dimensioni 3 x 3.2 m

RIPIANI A SCOMPARSA
apertura scorrevole

CAMERINO_DEPOSITO
armadi e contenitori
abiti su misura

PLAN | home   SCALA 1:50

KAO SOSPENSIONE
luce Artemide

PORTA IPAD

LED RGB

SPECCHIO A PARETE
dimensioni 3x3.2m

OUREA 156
Artemide

SPECCHIO
A PARETE

SCALA 1:50

a) Per cantare queste lacrime Finalmente
ho scoperto che io appartengo a questo posto

b) E ti ringrazio per avermi portato
qui Per avermi mostrato casa

c) Beh, io sto affogando nel
tempo per un battito disperato

APPENDIABITI
LAVORAZIONE DEL
FERRO SU MISURA

For singing these tears
finally I've found that I belong here

And I thank you for bringing
me here for showing me home

bringing
me here

ESPOSITORE IN LEGNO
FINITURA IN RESINA
X 3 elementi

E_TURN KUNDALINI
PANCA IN VETRO RESINA

SOGLIA IN PIETRA
GRIGIO SCURO

Well I'm drowning in time
to a desperate beat

ALZATO | parete sinistra

HORIZONTAL SHOWCASE

SERRANO + BAQUERO

The Olmedo building was built in Granada in 1953, hosting the first covered shopping gallery of the city. After giving cover to different businesses, a deterioration process began in a way that the entrances to the different shops turned into service back doors, closed permanently with metallic blinds. In 2010, the business placed at the inside corner of the gallery, the only one with no exit to the street, was leased to set a clothing shop. The available surface was really limited, just only 33 square metres, so a review of aspects such as the showcase was necessary.

The project was based on the revitalizing of the total gallery, starting with this shop, operation that was done with short means and a scale-limited action, but with a great impact due to its position. We proposed a subversion of the traditional concept of a showcase, exploring the possibility of blurring the limits between the private and the public areas of a clothing store.

In this way, we could create interchanges between spaces of different characteristics. The shop would give air, 24 hours of light to the gallery as well as an activity program able to attract visitors to the place: music sessions- the client is a well-known DJ- break dance exhibitions or showings. On the other hand, the shopping gallery would be temporarily occupied as an extension of those activities and the showing area of the store.

The strategy to materialize these objectives consisted of two actions: the enhancement of the discovered original elements of the building, recovering its identity and the building of a horizontal showcase, a glass pavement that hosts the clothing garments and the light, allowing the exhibition area to be a part of the gallery.

PHOTOGRAPHY: IÑIGO BEGUIRISTAIN & IÑAKI BERGERA
LOCATION: NAVARRA, SPAIN

TOP OUTLET STORE

IÑIGO BEGUIRISTAIN & IÑAKI BERGERA

Designed by Iñigo Beguiristain and Iñaki Bergera, Top Outlet Store is located in Av. de Pamplona 1, Pamplona, Navarra, Spain. The project has gained awards including WAN Retail International Award 2011, Longlisted, Interior Design COAVN Award 2010, First Price, Navarra Chamber of Commerce Design Special Award 2000-10, First Price, Navarra Chamber of Commerce Design Award 2009, First Price, Interior Design SALONI Award 2009, Finalist to name a few.

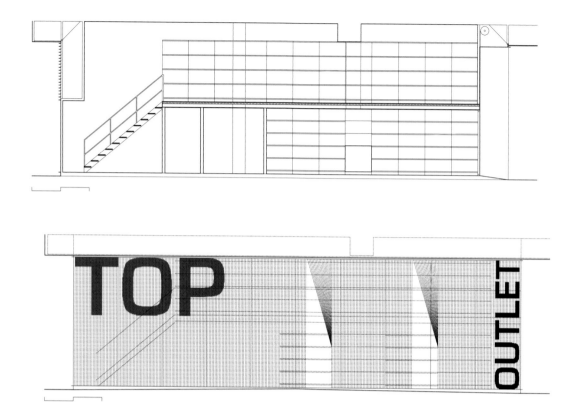

PLEATS PLEASE ISSEY MIYAKE TAIPEI THE MALL

KEISUKE FUJIWARA

KEISUKE FUJIWARA

The shop was planned simple as if the space shaved off from rectangular solid. Mannequins were placed on the shop front and the items were displayed at the hanger rack beside walls. Items with several colors are displayed on the shelves at the center of shop in order to show colors and feelings in each season.

The design elements for this space are "WHITE, GLOSS and LIGHT".

It may also say the space represented white colored canvas for painting. Displayed items with several colors become the elements to compose the attractive space design.

Indirect lights are installed to dimly light up on the walls. These soft lights represent calmness, while a bright light on shelves provide a power to the space. This balance of illuminance is important elements for the shop.

Floor, walls and furniture are finished with gloss material. The gloss reflects the color and shape of items, so that real image and virtual image appear. They express profundity or suggestiveness in the space.

The interior design for PLEATS PLEASE was aimed to have a feeling of modestly, instead of making the space with strong impression.

PHOTOGRAPHY: DAISUKE SHIMA / NACASA & PARTNERS INC.
LOCATION: TOKYO, JAPAN

ISSEY MIYAKE BLOOM BLOOM BLOOM

EMMANUELLE MOUREAUX

Issey Miyake commissioned Emmanuelle Moureaux to handle the set design and art direction for their event, "bloom bloom bloom". Inspired by spring flowers in bloom and Issey Miyake's newest incarnation, this event was held in conjunction with the launch of Bloom Skin, Yoshiyuki Miyamae's first collection since joining the branch as their new designer. The event took place at both Isetan's Shinjuku branch and Mitsukoshi's flagship store in Nihonbashi. These "Stick Flowers", with their straight lines and contours were conceived as a contrast to the translucent designs of the soft, flowing pieces in this collection. Each measuring 1.4m across, these vibrant and colorful flowers were deployed as both three-dimensional sculptural pieces and two-dimensional graphic motifs, giving the overall impression of a stage "in bloom". Stick Flower represents an extension of "sticks", a series of display windows designed by Emmanuelle for Issey Miyake's three Aoyama outlets, as well as "Toge", an installation she exhibited at Designtide Tokyo. For "bloom bloom bloom", Issey Miyake also commissioned Emmanuelle Moureaux to design logos and outdoor signs for the department store. The Stick Flower motifs were also used in a series of limited edition T-shirts and package designs for accessories and products. The combination of these vibrantly colored items and the fresh, vital space they were displayed in created a symphony of rich hues that perfectly complemented the new image of Issey Miyake.

bloom bloom bloom
ISSEY MIYAKE

3/7 wed. - 3 13 tue.

BAO BAO ISSEY MIYAKE
×
ISSEY MIYAKE

ESTNATION NAGOYA

MOMENT

ESTNATION mainly sells the clothes for both sexes. What the designers attempted is leaving the general idea, which means that the shop is normally divided into some zones by the walls. Here, the various furniture like sculptures vaguely partition the whole space, such as the metallic blue pillars, glued laminated timber counter, and sharp façade. They would gather the customers' attention, moreover the use of some colors in this simple space strongly appeals to them. They will hopefully lead the passersby into the shop, then they will be easy to walk inside without any wall partitions. What is important for the retail design is that letting them walk a lot and see the commodities to stimulate customers' psychology. It would be dull to divide clearly the space into ladies' and men's area by the walls, but the presence like a sculpture guides them and show where they are inside the shop with interest and curiosity.

ECKO UNTLD

STONE DESIGNS

Ecko represents the most rebel heart from NYC; it is the response to the adoption of bourgeois ways by fashion, the commitment with people on the streets that have made of NY the iconic city that represents to the rest of the world. This is why Ecko stores cannot be a standard commercial place. They have of course to comply with certain parameters that cannot be avoided but, at the same time, they can skip many rules that other brands cannot. For us, Ecko deserved a store image that got the feeling of the most authentic NY from the 80's and 90's, those years in which NY was a high-spirited city in which the most exciting social, artistic and cultural events had place. Our idea is to mix the best things from the past with the present New Yorker icons that will last in the future. . We want to show in a clear way how a city and a culture may have influenced our lives and how Ecko is a brand that has not only been influenced by NY, but which has also been part of it, has contributed to it and still contributes actively to keep it alive.

AND A YOKOHAMA

MOMENT

AND A YOKOHAMA

MOMENT

060

And A has a wide selection of men's and ladies clothes, accessories, shoes, bags, and household goods. Therefore the shop design should be open to welcome various targets. The shop is divided into two areas, light space at front and dark space at a back. White colored light area gives customers a casual and open image, so that they would be easy to come into the shop. At a glance, another area does not stand, but it draws their attention toward a back of the shop once they enter the shop, as "oh, there are more goods here than I expect."

The front white area also exists as a public area. It means that the pure white as a basic color has an illusion that as if it is the extension of the public passage. The designers are interested in the power of white color as no individuality. The designers additionally did not construct any interruptions around the facade and keep the entrance width as much as possible to make customers not feel hesitation to enter the shop. The easy step-in is the most important to design this shop because the designers should prepare many chances that customers touch the commodities anyhow to give success in sales.

After their steps, the red line running up to down, and left to right leads customers inside the shop deeper. This red, And A's main brand color, stands a lot in the white area. Once customers notice this line, they realize the they are already in And A, not in a public area.

Then, a dark area finally catches their eyes. The scene changes light to dark, thus their walk speed becomes slow, and it gives them a relaxed mood during shopping. These two different moods cause a rhythm for shopping. Moreover customers would enjoy the shift of the scenes among these. The designers also expect that these two different areas expand the possibilities of display as And A has a wide selection.

STORE MAYGREEN IN HAMBURG

KINZO

Owners Insa Riske and Mechthild Schilmöller commissioned the Berlin-based trio KINZO with their resolutely futuristic design for their first fashion boutique MAYGREEN. The store opened in the classy Hamburg neighbourhood of Ottensen. Freestanding white objects soaring close above the dark brown floor made of smoked oak. The polygonal chiseled appearance recalls the aesthetic of rugged chunks of pack ice. The objects bear reference to each other through their optical alignment evoking a tension in between. Functional details such as a cushion for seating or a display case in the counter are naturally integrated in the shape. A distinctive ducting of electrical cables covered in green textile sets the highlight on the ceiling: Every single cable leads to a source of light, either a directed spotlight or a glaring DNA pendent luminaire. Usually concealed, the cables start to become an impressive design element that visually refers to something like a vegetative circuit board. The delicate but oversized grasshopper has been laser cut in a customized perforation pattern. Backlit in green it forms the appropriate background for MAYGREEN's LOHAS (Lifestyle of Health and Sustainability) concept.

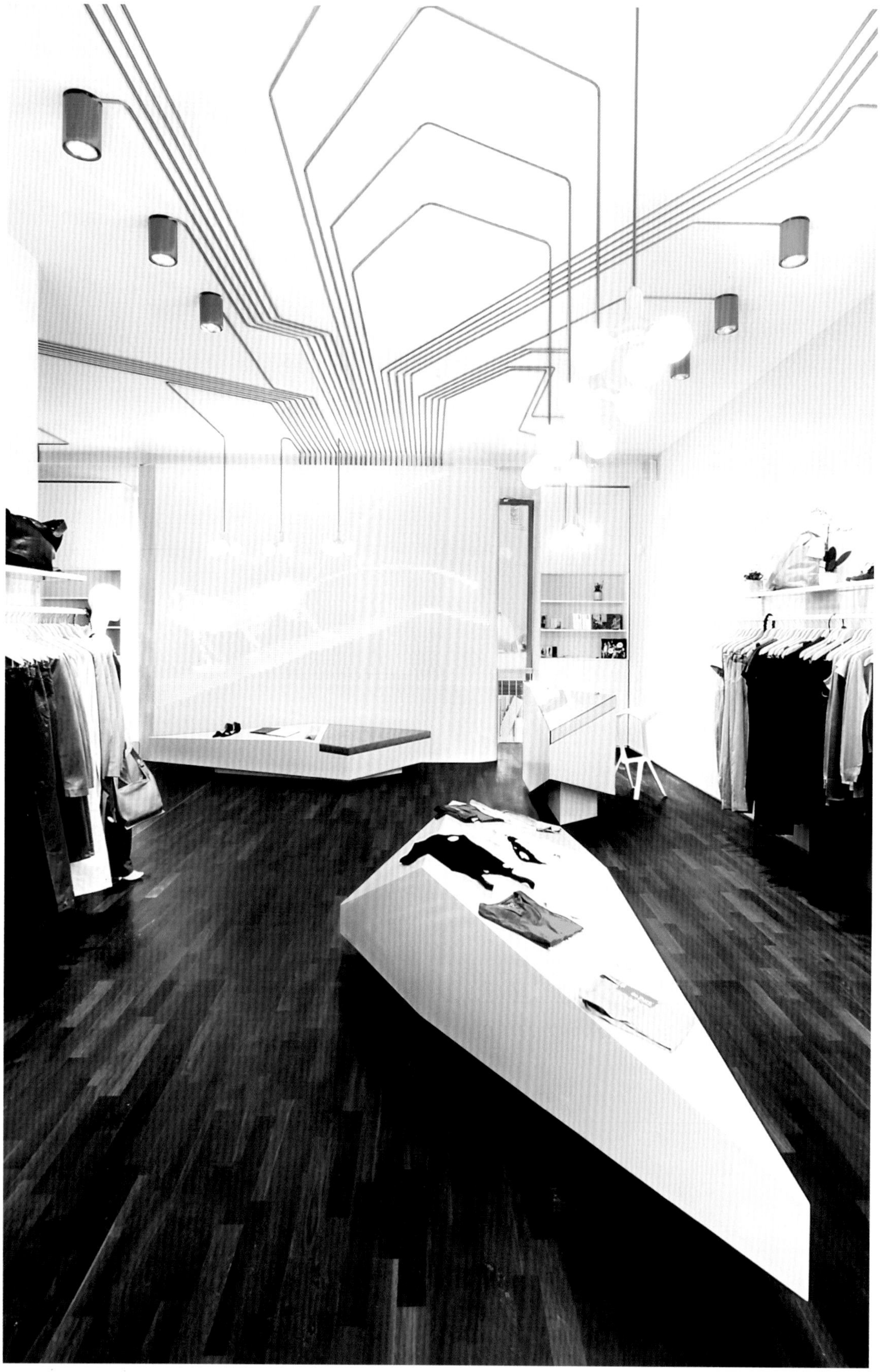

LARA KOFU

CHIKARA OHNO/SINATO

An apparel store for young women located in a train station mall in Kofu, Japan.

The site is on the ground floor and has facades facing both inside and outside. The designer wanted to make the best use of this condition and decided to divide the vertical space with a lattice plane which the separates the shop below and a void above while connecting the two facades without disrupting the view. At its lowest point it is 1320mm from the floor, at its highest stretching to 3000mm. Large openings in the lattice plane at its low point allow one to enter the lattice. By poking your head above the lattice plane, as if at the bottom of a valley, it creates a new experience in the space of the shop, perhaps softening it.

LARA KOFU

CHIKARA OHNO/SINATO

070

NOTE ET SILENCE. MINT KOBE

SPECIALNORMAL INC.

Note et silence is a select shop, which newly opened in Kobe, a port city in Kansai area. The shop holds three original brands, which appeal to sophisticated women with a sense of humor and with a playful mind. 'Humor' and 'Playfulness' was the key when the designers started this project, and they defined the shop as a stage, customers as actors / actresses, and the interior as a stage setting. 'Floating box' Wall, Floor and Ceiling are the main elements to create a space. Based on the idea of 'Stage Setting', the designers aimed to create a versatile space and they made Wall (= Box), can be moved to a certain extent. If the box is placed near the entrance, it creates a corridor and the space becomes very aggressive atmosphere. If it is placed at the back of the shop, it creates a bigger area within the shop. With the effect of the box, the space can be configured for different scenes like a gallery.

GRANADA CAMPER STORE

A-CERO

On Mesones street, one of the best known, commercial and important streets of Granada, Spain, there is a little store of 48 m² that has been renovated by A-cero. The customer is the Spanish leading brand Camper, devoted to the exhibition and sale of trendy shoes. It will be its first store in Granada. The first important point is the use of the space, as a wide and useful place is needed. A-cero was selected for this work because of its actual, fresh and dynamic design, the keys for Joaquín Torres and Rafael Llamazares projects.

Two colors: white and red, typical of the A-cero interior design projects and Camper. The space is open and projected with organic elements like the expositors, made of lacquered wood with white shelves and red face, having an indirect lighting by LEDs. Also, following the floor shapes, there is a red and white bolon. Adding more sculptural values to the complex, in the middle part there is another module curve used as a breach change. To achieve more depth at the rear wall there is a mirror. There is still a space for a warehouse at the back. The front is made of composite panel with red aluminum and the showcase has been made of glass and red vinyl following the style of the store. The final result is an interesting fusion between the corporative resources and designs of Camper and A-cero. A special place that improves the market of the area and also to feel the universe of Camper and A-cero.

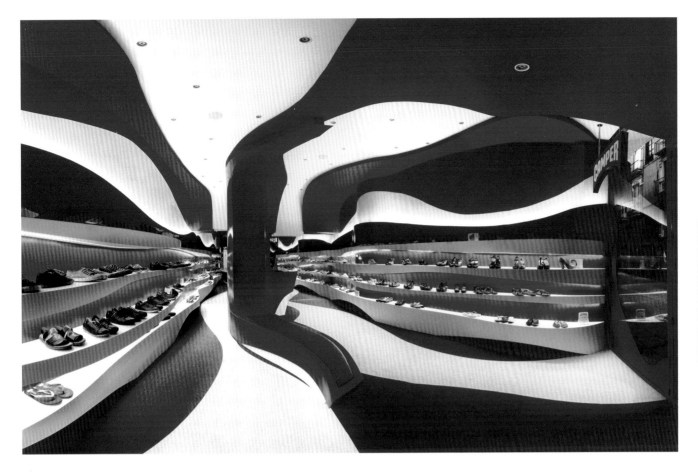

PLAJER & FRANZ STUDIO

SHOP ISABEL MARANT

CIGUË

Situated in a quiet street in the back of Omotesando Avenue in Tokyo, the shop reinvests a deserted house of the 70's. The main gesture was to reveal the wood structure of the second floor, as under construction, and trying to keep a part of the residential 'home feeling' it had.

The following fixture and furniture intervention tried to be minimal and subtle, in order to weave with the warm existing atmosphere.

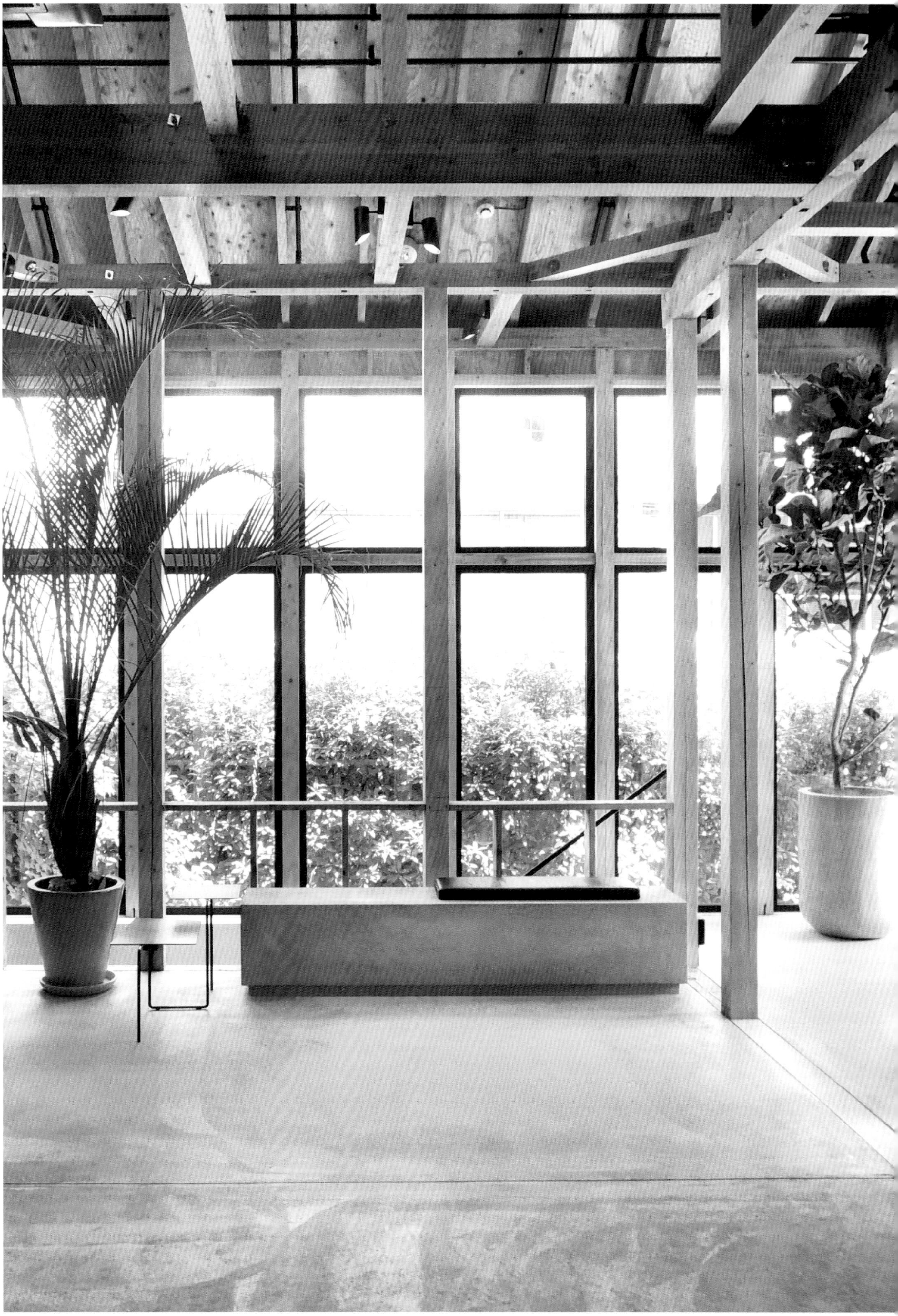

RAGEBLUE FUKUOKA

CHIKARA OHNO/SINATO

This project is for the conversion of the second and third story of a three-story retail building into a men's apparel shop. The client, who had already been operating out of the same location, wanted to draw attention to the entrance stairs from the road passing in front and thought that a method of 'guiding' was necessary to induce customer flow to the less efficient third floor sales area. A portion of the second floor sales area is pushed out over the exterior entrance stair so that part of the sales floor becomes a floating display. Here, the members supporting the clothes hanger pipe also have the structural role of suspending the floor beams of the cantilevered floor. Within the interior atrium, the designer suspended a new sales floor level at a height of 1.4m from the second floor level in order to offer a form of 'guidance', leading customers to the third floor.

The second floor has a story height of 3.8m, so it could be perceived as a burden to climb directly to the third floor level. However, the designer thought that movement to an intermediate level would seem relatively easy. By adding the additional level, the designer thought that the third floor would feel closer and be much easier to access. The intermediate floor is made of transparent glass and is suspended over an empty stainless finish floor. This floor diffusely reflects exterior light from the large facade aperture and creates a small clearing, offering a vivid contrast to the surrounding shop filled with merchandise.

PHOTOGRAPHY: BRENDAN AUSTIN
LOCATION: STOCKHOLM, SWEDEN

HOPE FLAGSHIP STORE

CHRISTIAN HALLERÖD & JOHAN LYTZ

Hope Flagship Store, Norrmalmstorg, Stockholm, Sweden. The store covering 140 m² has an air of industrialism and vintage. To achieve this effect there is a concrete floor, walls and tiles are white and visible ventilation. Lighting placed between ventilation drums in the ceiling enhances the raw and industrial character.

In contrast, there is a separate room that is sophisticated and pleasant, where one can sit down in peace and quiet. To attain a warmer tone, tailor-made pine joists and brush painted plywood were used. A big sliding door divides this space from the rest of the store. The glass for this door, the designer came across in the attic of a glazier's. The designer chose to use copper, solid wood and marble to create an atmosphere of both visual and tactile pleasure. In order to achieve the right finish and quality it is important for the designers to work with local cabinet-makers.

CHRISTIAN HALLERÖD & JOHAN LYTZ

HOPE

HABERDASH

FORM US WITH LOVE

Haberdash is the contemporary dandy store in Stockholm. Form Us With Love designed the interior for the newly opened shop at Upplandsgatan 50 in Stockholm. Form Us With Love approached the project by researching and selecting materials reflecting the level of detail and quality of Haberdash's fashion. The results is an interior with products from materials used in a new way, including Silestone quarts slabs for display wall and counter, Kährs ash flooring for display stands and leather remnants from tannery Tärnsjö for seating. The newly launched pendant glass lamps designed by Form Us With Love for Design House Stockholm frames the setting.

FORM US WITH LOVE

HABERDASH

FORM US WITH LOVE

109

WON HUNDRED STORE

ARCGENCY

Wouldn't it be great if the interior concept for a store could be flexible, easy repeatable and at the same time unique, high quality and true to the brands values? Creating this, was the ambition for the new Won hundred store. Instead of using a rigid modular system, the designers chose something that has the repetitive quality of a modular system, but with a more loose and playful attitude. The hollow wooden 'log' was the perfect choice. The 'logs' can be stacked, staggered and rotated, creating spaces on, between, in and under for displaying items. The 'logs' are made from pine and treated with a natural wax. They are a reinterpretation of Scandinavian style where craftsmanship, simple materials and a clean design is combined to create a look that is in line with the Won hundred brand.

The interior is designed exclusively for Won hundred. Often furniture and interior for shops are one-off's, created mainly to look and not to perform – just like props for a theatre play. The designers wanted to create real furniture that would stand the ware and tare, making it possible to recompose the interior, move elements from one shop to another and mix brand new elements with old. By making the interior elements both multifunctional and high quality, the lifespan of these are enhanced. For Arcgency resource awareness is a crucial design parameter. The designers believe that making better products that lasts longer will generate less waste. While being a sensible and sustainable solution to making store interior, it also creates a more appealing experience for the user.

ZALANDO POP UP STORE

SIGURD LARSEN DESIGN & ARCHITECTURE

Inspired by the large wooden crates used in the shipping industry, the design for Zalando's Pop-Up Store features three free-standing boxes, each revealing a separate collection. The boxes are placed at angles to the concrete walls, guiding the visitor through the space as they discover the assorted rooms of the furniture. Concrete stools echo the materiality of the walls, and act as counterweights for the hangers of a fourth collection. Prior to the opening of the Pop Up Store, stacks of white boxes used by the company to distribute goods covered the windows. Over time the facade of white boxes will disintegrate, revealing the content of the shop day by day.

BETULLA STORE

CAROLA VANNINI ARCHITECTURE

Interior design project of a clothing store located in the Campo de' Fiori area, the heart of Rome's historical center. The store renovation included the complete reorganization of interior spaces, as well as the design of new accessories and lighting.

The Betulla store is a wide space where fashion meets architecture. Clothes, colors and materials all melt in order to create a magic flair that reminds of northern lands. Grey concrete and rough wood cover the walls while contrasting with the floor's total white. Clothes, shoes and other items are arranged in a unique way, as if they were exposed in an art gallery space. Clothes are hung on an iron structure and look like precious sculptures emphasised by the rough walls veneering. The final purpose of this modern boutique's project was to create a private and comfortable space, just like somebody's personal wardrobe.

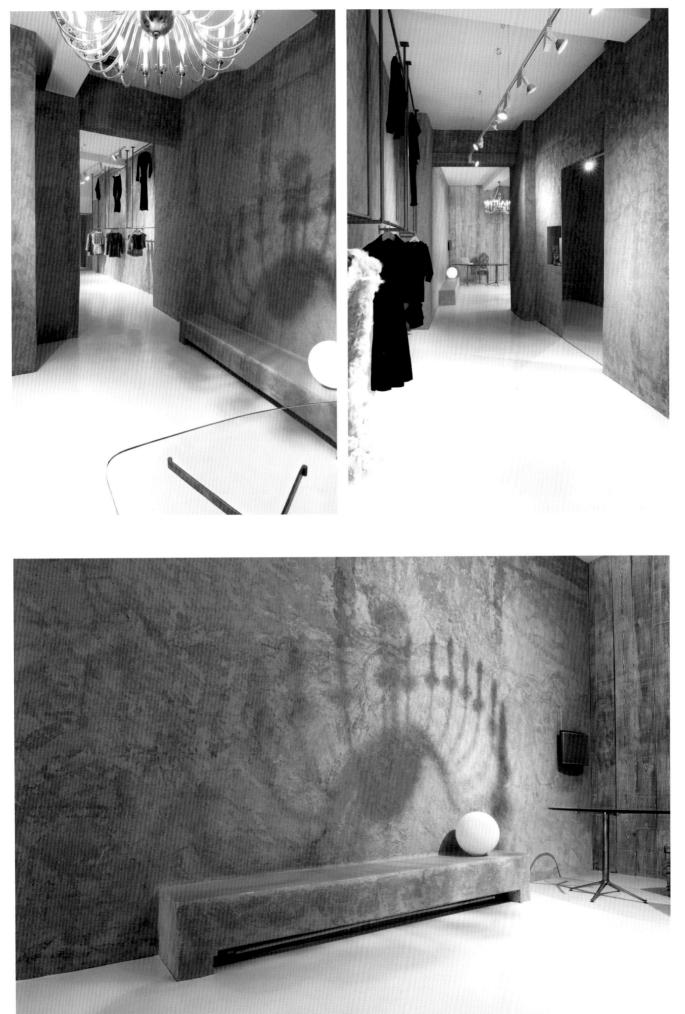

L'ECLAIREUR

SAQ

This is not just a shop; it's a fantasy in which everyone has to find a story for themselves. Within the idiom of L'Eclaireur, shoppers are guests and are genuinely welcomed as such by every staff member. Adapted to his/her wishes and interest, the guest is proposed a personalized visit and in so-doing discovers the exposed goods. Here, within a retail environment that would normally highlight merchandise, the visitor plays a privileged role in the act of its 'unveiling'.

More than two tons of recycled wooden planks, cardboard and used aluminum print-plates were delivered to shape the scenography of this haute-couture women's boutique. Paradoxically, the space seems weightless. The interior is conceived by the perimeter the sculptured walls follow to envelope the space. Though composed of recycled material, the final aspects of these walls have a stunning luxurious aspect. The effect is not only visual but also tactile and puts the first-time visitor off-guard.

Like an intimate dressing, this shop shatters the normal codes of « retail »: the curiosity of the visitor is triggered by the unconventional way of exposing or deliberate non-exposing of the goods. Each designer piece is a singular story which waits to be told and is housed in its own individual closet or alcove alongside diverse 'objets trouvés' or art-pieces.

Along the visitor's path, every area in the overall space, even though identical in components, differs in atmosphere through the interaction of wall-texture and ambient light. At the end of his or her route, the visitor enters the back area where, apparently, no product is exposed. Only the space enlightened by the sky domes and the video-installation reveal there is something more going on. Until the walls open up upon command.

DELAY

DESIGN OFFICE DRESS INC.

DELAY by Win & Sons is the fashion brand, owned by the company which is famous for their denim finishing technique. Their target clients are men, around 20-30 years-old, bad guy looks in their fashion. The designers designed this store like the factory, and also like the space, where those bad guys want to hang out at. By use of rough materials, iron and vintage finishing to each element of the space, the designers could successfully express the spirit of the brand.

DESIGN OFFICE DRESS INC.

129

DELAY

DESIGN OFFICE DRESS INC.

130

INTERIOR DESIGN OF WDSG ART & CRAFT DEPARTMENT

WUDAI SHIGUO

WDSG Art & Craft Dept. is continuously advocate the value of The Roots Of Style, an attitude of backing to the basic and tracing back to the roots. A combination of classic and characteristic design which has been taken back all the marvelous elements from the past to now. All the design details are rooted in timeless values and a rich heritage.

Under the dim lighting, a brass plaque engraved with WDSG Art & Craft Dept. logo is embedded in the rough bricks wall along the steep slope of St. Francis Street. A pair of intricate wrought iron floor grates gives intriguing glimpses into the basement shop below. A metal inscribed ceiling is embellished with floral pattern. The upstairs level of the shop to be classy, with wooden flooring and an old but elegant feel. The comparison of the lighter scheme to the upstairs, the mood is much more sombre. The walls are painted dark but shiny, because in the past, this was the color of the subways. In order to create a revolutionary ambience. There is a private meeting room that could have been used for plotting rebellions. Within that back room, a custom-made sliding wooden door and pivoting windows with wooden panels increase its mystery. Down a flight of stairs, terra-cotta hexagon floor tiles which laid into the concrete floors. Vintage leather sofas and armchairs against labels such as Los Angeles based Mr. Freedom and RRL, a niche collection by Ralph Lauren. To epitomize vintage sense of style, the selection is hanging on the rusty iron racks. Scented organic candles by Australian brand Plain & Simple makes good use of brown glass apothecary jars. They are also displayed on the metallic shelves. Lightings with their brass cages and fabric covered wiring feel raw and industrial.

The bygone look of the store is dedicated to those who believe in originality. The Roots of Style is the brand's theme. You don't have to just look forward for innovation, in looking back, you can find many things in our heritage to celebrate.

Creative Direction: Kenji Wong @ Wudai Shiguo
Art Direction & Design: Ahman Tang @ Wudai Shiguo
Text: Spancer Tang @ Wudai Shiguo

14 OZ. STORES

S1 ARCHITEKTUR

The idea is to establish 14 oz. Stores to be the first addresses in premium denim and high-end street & urban wear. The motto: "quality first", quality in the sense of service and "honest" products following the manufactory philosophy and stand representative for tradition, high-quality fabrics and first-class workmanship, authenticity and handicraft. 14 oz. does focus on manufacturers who follow ethical and sustainable manufacturing methods. 14 oz. stands for clothing culture and style – here, one would buy a wardrobe which lasts, beyond fast moving fashion trends.

14 oz. puts great emphasis on service and this accentuates the high quality standard. Well-trained, friendly sales personnel are able to give qualified information on the history and the special features of each brand. The overall concept has been conceived by S1 Architektur, Berlin in collaboration with Luis Mock, Rott am Inn. The architecture as well as the coherent environment is essential to 14 oz. The landmarked "Haus Cumberland" at Berlin's famous Kurfürstendamm hosting the 2nd 14 oz. subsidiary was built in 1911/1912 by the German architect Robert Leibnitz who was also responsible for the planning of world-famous Hotel Adlon. Named after the 3rd Duke of Cumberland Ernst August, the history-charged building has been refurbished true to original since 2011.

The interior of 14 oz. is fully tailored to its historical "shell": the former Art Nouveau archive library of Vienna's Palais Liechtenstein is the centerpiece. It dates back to the end of the 19th/beginning of the 20th century. The wood and steel elements were reprocessed with much love to detail and custom-fitted into the space. Antique furniture – like a French jeweler vitrine or wooden tables from the University of Liège (Belgium) from the 20ies – as well as modern classics like the Knoll sofa – complement this interior highlight in a classy way.

PHOTOGRAPHY: STUDIO ROBIN SLUIJZER
LOCATION: THE NETHERLANDS

COURT SEJOUR BOUTIQUE

ROBIN SLUIJZER

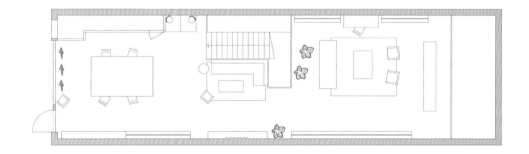

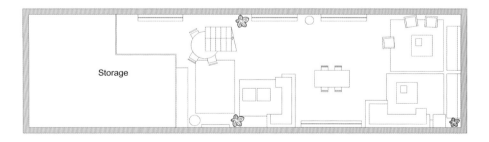

Storage

Court Sejour Boutique is a multi-brand lifestyle POP UP-store that offers those special people who like to inspire and get inspired a crispy, thrilling and conscientious selection of the finest in fashion, interior and art. It pops up at dazzling and temporary locations in the trend decisive cities of the world. One moment it will rock your soul with creative workshops and special events and the other moment it is gone, waiting for you to re-open the new crib. Court Sejour Boutique started her journey in Amsterdam. Studio Robin Sluijzer wanted to create a cozy, warm and homely environment where people could shop and relax.

LARA KANAZAWA

CHIKARA OHNO/SINATO

LARA is an apparel store for young women in a shopping mall located in Kanazawa Japan. The store has a very narrow frontage onto the passage of a shopping mall. The space turns to the right just a few steps inside from the frontage and has a deep space after it. Such an L-shaped site is difficult to use as an apparel store. The most important thing for the project was to bring people deep inside the store. The designer found that the wall facing the frontage was comparatively big in relation to the rest of the store, so he wanted to make the best use of it. The designer decided to make the wall with seven layers; six of expanded metal with different meshes and one mirrored wall behind these. Three layers of the expanded metal surface on the store-side pull away from the wall, becoming curved walls which receive people from the frontage. The expended metal produces a very complicated pattern when it is layered. However, when it curves and stands as a single wall, it changes its qualities becoming a guiding line which leads people inside the store without obstructing the view of the whole interior. The wall changes its pattern and depth as the surface layers pull away.

PHOTOGRAPHY: YOSHIRO MASUDA
LOCATION: OSAKA, JAPAN

NOT WONDER STORE

REIICHI IKEDA

This is an interior design for a clothing store and an atelier of the fashion brand "wonderland" in Osaka, Japan. On the first visit of the designer, what made him feel as if it is outside even though there was the ceiling was that there wasn't an entrance to define the border. The designer made it a point to keep this strange and unique feeling, and tried making new interiors. He did not simply change the interior design to a radically new one, but maximized the effect of the existing elements.

People very differently picture a world behind a closed door. So, by setting up an entrance at the unimagined point, the designer expected a favorable effect on the "shift of the border". The area made by the shift of the border gets you a bit confused, and you will lose the idea where you are, in or out. As a result, you find yourself coming in the shop.

LEVI'S FLAGSHIP STORE

CHECKLAND KINDLEYSIDES

CK's relaunch of Levi's® UK Flagship store on Regent Street, is a demonstration of Levi's® craftsmanship.

Designed as a journey through an artisan's working environment, a 'courtyard' transition space will showcase exclusive product collaborations and art exhibitions. Through two sets of huge factory doors visitors enter the main body of the store, which has a clean and industrial look and feel. Along the left hand wall, running over the stairwell, is the product gallery; this cowl paneling is inspired by textile inspection cabinets, and provides a canvas where seasonal and promotional product stories can be told.

Follow the contemporary glass staircase, down to the basement and the 'Inspection Room' where key fits and finishes are displayed on tailor's forms and in illuminated cabinets. The basement also houses the 501® Jeans warehouse. Here, customers will find different washes of the original button fly jean, with the 501® Jeans table to the center floor presenting the most popular finishes in an easy to shop display. The re-crafted flagship store is designed to demystify what makes one pair of Levi's® distinctly different from another – and that of its competitors – whilst easing the buying process for customers. "With this store Levi's® is aiming to offer its customers the ultimate brand experience. It is visually captivating whilst providing expert knowledge, product offering and storytelling. CK has created a place where craftsmanship and authenticity deliver the most genuine experience of the brand in Europe."

'LEVI'S®' stitched on both sides of tab.
'501Z' zipper version is introduced.
The term 'Overalls' is replaced by 'jeans'.

'Preshrunk' jeans are introduced.
Back rivets are removed.
Lowercase 'e' replaces capital 'E' on tab.
Prewashed 501® jeans first offered in
stonewash finish.
Innovative TV commercials for 501® jeans
featuring classic American soul music
mixed with nostalgia and romance, launched
in Europe.
Levi's® Vintage Clothing is launched, a
collection which faithfully reproduces
products from the archive in San Francisco.
In the same year that marks the
the company's 150th anniversary, and the
150th anniversary of the invention of
jeans, the Levi Strauss & Co. archives
acquires the world's oldest pair of 501®
jeans, which date to c1879.
LS&CO. collaborates with artist Damien
Hirst to create 501® jeans in his famous
Spin Art style.
501® jeans for women are introduced
as the original boyfriend fit.
The 501® jeans warehouse is installed in
this store, to celebrate the world's most
iconic jean.

NIKE X LIBERTY RUNNING COLLECTION

HOTEL CREATIVE

The brand new Nike X Liberty running collection fuses sport and style in the most progressive collaboration to date. Featuring the edgy Lotus Jazz Liberty print, this dynamic women's range includes lifestyle silhouettes as well as Nike+ enabled shoes, to explore a futuristic journey of Nike Running from pure performance to explosive style.

Timed to celebrate a key sporting moment in time, revolutionary technology renders the running models super-lightweight and with a sleeker fit than ever before. While neon contrast styling vaults across the collection to give both running and fashion footwear (the iconic Nike Air Max 1; Air Force 1, Vintage Blazer and Nike Dunk Basketball styles) a directional design lift. And to complement the footwear collection, 24 limited edition Nike X Liberty Destroyer Jackets are available in two styles in-store.

If you're an athlete in training, or addicted to the gym these are sure to aid your performance and your style.

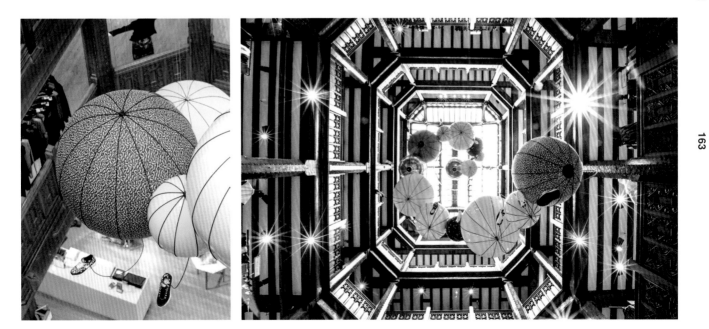

PHOTOGRAPHY: PIYAWUT SRISAKUL
LOCATION: BANGKOK, THAILAND

VELA DE

ALL(ZONE)

A small boutique in the stylish neighborhood of Bangkok, Vela De, aims to blend and stand out of the chaotic urban fabric at the same time, day and night. Hanging from above, the display of the dresses mainly attracts eye sights by moving vehicles. Glass, reflective metal, mirror help to create an interior space which is also merged with an urban space, as if the dresses are floating in a small street.

BEL ÉTAGE

PHILIP JIN HONERMANN / AVENUE A

From the inside of bar suite 212, a dark steel crafted, solid state staircase leads to the upper 120 sqm boutique loft. The brass finished custom made light structure generates a glamorous touch while entering first floor, which used to be a club many years ago.

Rough abraded concrete floor is covered in grey Epoxy casting, while smooth unflustered jet black ceiling and walls back out, to dispose impact to the different wall textures like French metro tiles or drapes made of finest Italian silk.

Custom made mobile product displays inspired by luggage trolley's, in combination with vintage design furniture joined by Kelim carpets, are placed to create a sophisticated but delightful atmosphere.

Oversized illuminated black and white Helvetica letters placed in front of the large glass sheet facing the high street, generate communication into urban space

BIASA SHOP JAKARTA

GIOVANNI D'AMBROSIO / PT GREEN DESIGN

The project of the Biasa Showroom is grafted onto a confined and long lot and it is developed on four floors. The first two floors are Boutique while the upper two floors are for the Art Gallery.

The main expressive point is the reinforced concrete staircase in the heart of the boutique. It is realized with a series of elements. These elements are profiles with a rectangular section folding up following a G shape. They have been realized on site in reinforced concrete in different heights following the height of the steps. The upper part of the G profile is the step of the staircase, while the lower one becomes the exhibition of the shop.

It's not a traditional staircase anymore. It follows this idea of mixing two different functions, the vertical connection and exhibition. Moreover this staircase is standalone by the structural point of view, because it is not connected to the wall, but each G element sustains itself.

The strength of the staircase is doubled by a bronzed mirror wall, 23 meters long for a total of 125 square meters, which amplified the space and contains useful hidden wardrobes for the shop.

The Art gallery space is characterized by an open space with a mixing of materials like clear concrete, wood and terpal, a plastic and cheap material used in rice fields by the Indonesian farmers here applied in volumes hanged on ceiling to hide the main lighting of the staircase to these floors.

PHOTOGRAPHY: PASCAL MONTARY
LOCATION: PARIS, FRANCE

IDEAL TOWER

SOME

The customer is a young designer of talent who launches its first collection. She recovered a small workshop of the Basfroi Street, Paris XI°, previously occupied by ironmongers, to make her first shop of it. The room is not exploitable in the state, and the former occupants can't imagine this place will be able one day to sell fashion articles. When Blanche exposes her attempts, the designers immediately understand that her needs are not only one shop, but also all the functions that a company needs to live: an office, a room conference, a workshop, storage and the conveniences which go with. Everything in 35m², and with a very tight budget rather.

For the designers' greater happiness, the project will not be summarized to draw 2 racks, to supervise the painter and to establish the catches. Quite to the contrary, the designers gonna speak program, cuts, details, structure, circulations – Showing that there is not small project and that architecture can nest in the most modest orders. As it is precisely the first order, the designers adopt a radical posture. The designers propose a tower… a high-rise office building inside the room. The proposal surprises the client, but after all why not. The designers have to see large and modesty does not have its place in Business. This tower will gather all the conveniences necessary to the operation of its company and will release a maximum of surface for the showroom. To stick to the budget, the designers knew that it would be necessary to work with a small company which would be not expensive. These kinds of companies which are confronted to the wild competition of the rehabilitation of small Parisian flat market. No carpenter, nor metal worker. Simply motivated craftsmen bus amused by the object to build.

LE CIEL BLEU

NORIYUKI OTSUKA

A white space in brilliant colors. It is a luxurious architectural space of about 278 m^2 with a ceiling 5m high. When approaching the design, Noriyuki Otsuka simultaneously embraced the two opposing notions of the overall concept as well as the detailed design of the space. The designer was conscious that if he based his design on the functional requirements of the space such as the number of products that could be housed, he would end up with an interior resembling a fashion retail megastore. The design that he proposed was an interior space which incorporated another architectural space within it. This interior space was a cylinder made with a structurally self-supporting mesh. Because of the size of the feature the designer wanted to avoid integrating it too much with the surrounding space, so deliberately aligned it off center from the axis of the building. This layout gives the space a sense of gravity. The designer also included custom-made hanging light fittings in his plan for the cylinder in order to make the interior space the central focus of the design.

CROCODILE TOKYO

CHIKARA OHNO/SINATO

Crocodile is an apparel store for young women in a shopping mall located in Tokyo Japan. The store has a very narrow frontage onto the passage of a shopping mall. The space turns to the right just a few steps inside from the frontage and has a deep space after it. Such an L-shaped site is difficult to use as an apparel store. The most important thing for the project was to bring people deep inside the store. I found that the wall facing the frontage was comparatively big in relation to the rest of the store, so I wanted to make the best use of it. We decided to make the wall with seven layers; six of expanded metal with different meshes and one mirrored wall behind these. Three layers of the expanded metal surface on the store-side pull away from the wall, becoming curved walls which receive people from the frontage. The expended metal produces a very complicated pattern when it is layered. However, when it curves and stands as a single wall, it changes its qualities becoming a guiding line which leads people inside the store without obstructing the view of the whole interior. The wall changes its pattern and depth as the surface layers pull away.

CHIKARA OHNO/SINATO

192

LINEA PIU

KOIS ASSOCIATED ARCHITECTS

The project is the creation of Linea Piu Boutique in Mykonos Island. Mykonos is part of the Cyclades islands complex renowned for its elegance and exuberant lifestyle. The cube-shaped buildings and whitewashed exterior facades, the meandering roads that twist through the main city of Chora, the beautiful churches and the windmills compose an imagery that is characteristic and emblematic of Greece and the Mediterranean beauty.

Allusion is the concept of the new boutique in Mykonos Island, allusion to the Grecian myth and tradition that saturates the Aegean. The structure and all the original architectonic elements were preserved and within this clean historic shell the new fittings and furniture were surgically fitted into place. The selection of objects reflects various aspects of the island, and connects us to its history. The custom made iron furniture and fittings allude to beautiful ancient findings of the Mykonos Museum and their texturing is reminiscent of the texturing found on Alberto Giacometti sculptures. The installation in the dress display room alludes to the diffused mellow light that the Mykonian shutters introduce to an interior space. The polyhedral lamps make the designers think the Mykonos old lighthouse and the tranquil strolls by the sea. The elegant leather stools travel the designers to the traditional Mykonian meeting places like the square and the yard. The whole synthesis is orchestrated in a way that wakes up memory and brings to mind images from the life of the island. It is routed to the place in a contextual manner but not a scenographic one. The designers' goal was to synthesize a space the combines the brand's aesthetic and design clarity, quality and finesse and is nor isolated nor detached from its location and spirit of the place.

PHOTOGRAPHY: TAMAS BUJNOVSZKY
LOCATION: BUDAPEST, HUNGARY

NANUSHKA FLAGSHIP STORE

DANIEL BALO, ZSOFI DOBOS, DORA MEDVECZKY, JUDIT EMESE KONOPAS, NOEMI VARGA

Nanushka is a fashion store in Budapest with a billowed canvas canopy and a sliced firewood floor. The young Hungarian fashion designer Sandra Sandor handpicked a team of enthusiastic graduates after posting an ad in several design schools. Working together for the first time, Daniel Balo, Zsofi Dobos, Dora Medveczky, Judit Emese Konopas andNoemi Varga hoisted 250 square meters of fabric into place around the walls and ceiling of the shop for clothing brand Nanushka. In three weeks, the collective fashioned a space in which the previous interior has been left intact.

The interior of the store is warm and rugged. The ceiling of the interior is 80 square meters of linen and cotton is draped by a rigging system. The soft fabric is accented by firewood and rusted steel details. Firewood is sliced into small circles, then securing these elements to the ground, by which the floor construction for the retail unit was accomplished. There are also small display stands formed from bundles of logs, clothing racks made from rusted steel contrast the softness of the linen drapery of the walls and ceiling. The organic aesthetic is enhanced by spherical lanterns hanging from the ceiling. White linen poufs mirroring the shape of the lanterns are grouped around the store interior for store goers to rest upon.

MEMORY NINO ALVAREZ, SHOP OF MULTIMARKS

RIFE DESIGN

Nino Alvarez is a women's fashion shop with the leading trademarks situated in the centre of San Cugat. It has a space of about 90 m² with a very long narrow structure with two entrances with natural light, one direct on the front wall and the other indirectly from the courtyard. The type of place determines from the beginning the idea of the design or plan.

The entrance to the shop is framed in the façade by a box of painted iron sheet except the difference between the street level and the shop and creating a gradual change between the outside and the inside completely visible. In this way all the front wall is glass, including the automatic door that shuts the shop, getting a complete view of the space from the street. The showcase is completed by two pieces of differentiated properties one product more specific and the other more conceptual. The arrangement of the pieces in the inside is not purely casual, studying the transition of the flow of people. It has the whole wall of smoked glass on one of the two sides of the premises in a way that it reflects on this glass the rest of the elements in the shop giving at the same time a greater illumination and it also amplifies the space. The mirror is the protagonist of the shop. Through this wall with the wavy and zig zag lines one is invited to visit it. It is carried out in various plans of this material assembled on a prior framework. The different gaps that originate between the changes of the plan are taken advantage of, as a niche to display clothes and accessories. The reflection of this wall in the roof is a big cut of a dark background that permits this to fall in its interior.

EG10

RIFE DESIGN

These two business premises are located in the basement of the Hotel Gran Palas and Palas in Pineda (Tarragona). Relatively near each other, the two boutiques have been designed with black-stained oak wood.

The leading element of the design of both stores is the lighting. One of them is in a horizontal plane on the roof and in the other, in a vertical plane in one of the walls. This backlight system allows graduate color, graduation and intensity of light. The graduation of the light gets an optimal point to illuminate products. In the case of the backlit in vertical wall, it is accompanied by a metal structure that functions as a counter to hang, bend and display. This game of metallic tubular structure lines creates a system of organization with much movement.

In both places, products are stored in the structure, this way there is no specific area of storage. The space for this purpose is situated in the upper part of the hangers. This module of cabinets is designed with wooden panels of different levels that hide the openings of the cabinets, which are camouflaged-stained oak. Also in the two boutiques are designed central volumes that serve as displays and containers, and one of them even of cash register. The structures are not too high, which allows seeing the entire store. Fitting rooms have been integrated into the wooden structure to ensure that they do not stand out or charge unnecessary attention. The two sideboards are designed of the same wooden structure, which extends up to the ground or is suspended, creating an interesting visual sensation from the outside. The pavement has been resolved with a dark textile floor.

TIPS FASHION STORE

///BYN
NICOLAS SALTO DEL GIORGIO & BITTOR SANCHEZ-MONASTERIO

TIPS Fashion Store is located on the ground floor of an old French Mansion in the heart of the former French Concession of Shanghai. The preexistence of the historic residential environment drove the design. The house is protected as well as all the existing details inside. The Store is located in the former dining and living room of the house, which kept the original woodworks, moldings, fire places, wood beams… The design had to be a contemporary contrast within that classical ambience, respecting the existing but drastically changing the appearance of the site.

The store is a multi-brand store and the designers needed to give a designated space for each designer's garments. The designers decided to create a series of freestanding bodies that will hold the entire new program. They are composed by a series of pods that hold the hanging units and the storage and a long desk for display and point of sale. All the new pods were produced in a factory from the 3d model and moved into the site, where they were installed in just 2 days minimizing the onsite work time. They are made in a folded 2.5mm metal plate and baked paint. The geometry of the pods and the connections between them drastically transformed the space enhancing some of the old details and covering others. The air conditioning, sound system and ambient lighting are hidden behind the pods.

FERRER STORE

SAQ

The assets of this multi-brand fashion store are based on both the singularity and exclusivity of the exposed collections and accessories. Each season-break is a period of thorough selection for a boutique that seeks unique fashion pieces, both excellent and sophisticated as adventurous and experimental.

For its spatial concept, SAQ decided to adopt these same criteria's. A careful selection of materials was essential to acquire an atmosphere structured by contrasts. Here raw meets refined, versatile meets sober, basic meets rich, and soft meets rough. The size and disposition of this shop is preserved thanks to the introduction of various 'textile islands' on the one hand and the light colored physical borders of the space on the other hand. Whereas the first allure and structure, the second reveal only discretely their presence and their custom-made skin.

The islands form a dotted pattern around which one circulates, they are a welcome visual and physical break in the client's shopping promenade. They also offer the opportunity to exchange or explore in a more private way the exclusive creations and accessories on display. In front of the vitrine, the hanging gardens of yarns ornamented with crystals lure the shopper inside.

BRIDAL MAGIC

TAO THONG VILLA + PROCESS5 DESIGN

Many people of all nationalities throng the main street that leads from JR Himeji Station to the World Heritage Site of Himeji Castle. Dress shop "Bridal Magic" is located in a side street just off this main street and was planned as a related facility in anticipation of the wedding hall that will face on to the main street.

The floor plan was created so that fitting rooms are located in the middle of the space and reception, waiting and dress display spaces are arranged around these. All four walls surrounding the fitting rooms are mirrored and randomly inlaid with frames. Some of these frames simply contain mirrors but others contain displays of accessories, apertures, lighting equipment and handles for the fitting room doors. This use of space surprises customers and creates an encounter with a stunning dress. This dress shop evokes the feelings of expectation and exaltation of the bride, who is the center of attention, with respect to her wedding.

TAO THONG VILLA + PROCESS5 DESIGN

USCARI SYDNEY

GREG NATALE DESIGN

Uscari is a raw, effortlessly sophisticated new fashion label. The flagship store design retains a certain restrained elegance, with minimal but impeccable detail. The few materials used, FC board, brick and galvanized metal tube, are inserted in unexpected ways to create an edgy space where the juxtaposition of soft fabrics seems only natural. The strong geometric elements are echoed throughout the store and resemble dangerous shards of broken mirror or a sharp lapel. The lighting creates a dramatic catwalk theatre effect accentuating the strong textural differences.

PHOTOGRAPHY: JIMMY COHRSSEN
LOCATION: FRANCE

MAISON MOYNAT PARIS

CURIOSITY

Gwenael Nicolas has been commissioned to direct/ as Director of the graphic and architectural design of Moynat, the illustrious French malletier (trunk maker) founded in Paris in 1849. One of the oldest malletiers, this historic brand was recently revived by Bernard Arnault and opened its new boutique, in Paris. The boutique is an invitation to travel through the circular space that encircles the column. The floor, composed of a titanium-coated glass mosaic, reflects light with a water-like effect. As you move through the different areas, the Moynat collection is revealed, with new products presented next to the original ones in a constant dialogue.

Carefully crafted lighting emphasizes each item to reveal the subtlety of textures and detailing. The display shelves are crafted from refined materials – washed French oak with leather trim – in a composition of vertical lines from floor to ceiling. The oak flooring fans out from the centre, inviting us to step further in. While the ground floor is an open space, the mezzanine offers a more intimate environment, with a salon, a gallery and the men's collection. The space opens to a large counter for special orders, lit by the glass ceiling, and an open salon with custom-designed sofas inspired by the curves of the trunks. Unique, historical trunks created by Moynat through the ages are presented in a gallery framed by the original "Havane" color of the brand. As you move through the space, it evokes curiosity to discover the history of the house and the excellence of the craftsmanship.

CURIOSITY

227

HERMÈS FLAGSHIP STORE

RDAI

Hermes inaugurated its new headquarters in Geneva, Switzerland. This is a stone building erected in 1946 by Marc Joseph Saugey, a prominent architectural figure in Geneva. Located near the lake, between the Rue du Rhone, Robert Street and the dock Céard General Guisan, the building raises seven levels, three of which are reserved for retail spaces.

Covering an area of 500 m², this new space reflects the spirit of RDAI, the Parisian architecture agency, responsible for the design of Hermes stores worldwide. Punctuated with tall windows, the rationalist inspired building of travertine shows great clarity. On the ground floor, six dark grey metallic framed showcases and decorated with Greek motifs at the base form large transparent show windows.

Perfectly symmetrical, the main entrance, rue du Rhône is framed by two large windows with slightly rounded corners in reference to the 24 Faubourg in Paris. The entry that opens onto a mosaic floor inlaid with the ex libris of 'la Maison, invites discovery of a first space devoted to silk, perfumes and accessories. It is balanced with a rhythm of clear Marmorino surfaces and chevron etched mirrors, which diffract light onto surfaces and volumes. The ties display incites the visitor to continue to the world of men, on the lakeside, which provides bespoke collection, leather, luggage and shoes. The ensemble is punctuated by glass furniture and cherry wood, and the '26/28 Faubourg Saint-Honoré' collection of seating in brown leather, designed by RDAI.

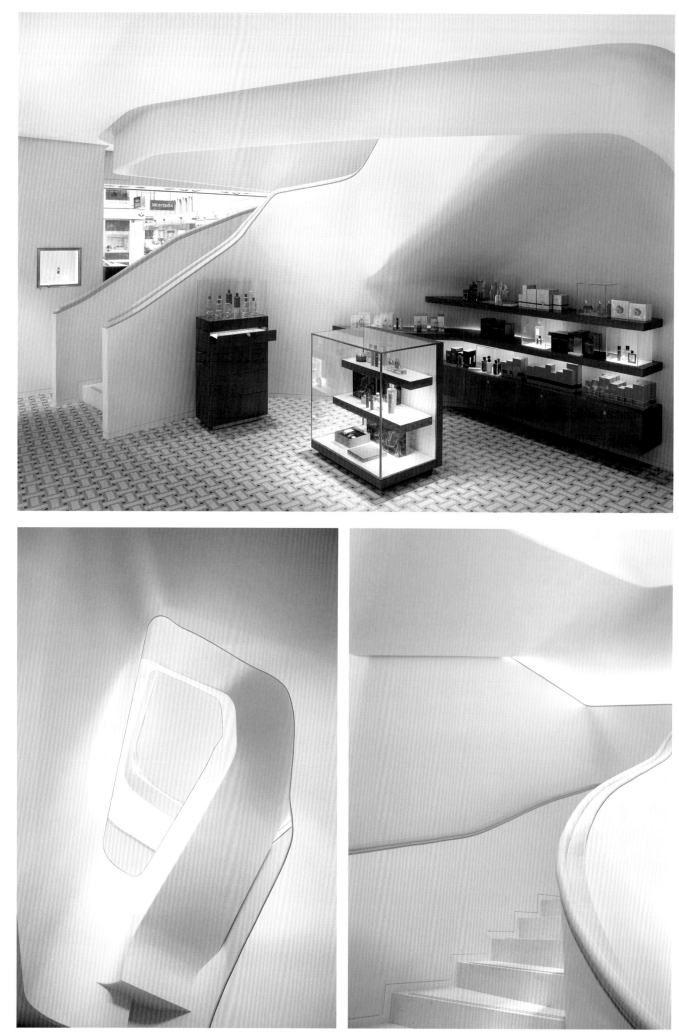

INDEX

A-CERO
SPAIN

Joaquin Torres and Rafael Llamazares constitute the architecture team known as A-cero. The key of A-cero work is to keep the theme of the idea throughout the whole process, from start to the crucial phase of the project management. In this sense, the "why" is as important as the "how." The project must be developed based on the more general concept to complete the definition of the smallest detail that materializes.

A-cero is currently experiencing a significant internationalization process, with projects in Europe, UAE, Lebanon, Russia, Saudi Arabia, and the US.

www.a-cero.com

ACNE
SWEDEN

Founded in Stockholm in 1996 by four creatives, Acne's ambition was to create and develop a lifestyle brand through the production of desirable products as well as helping others build their brands. This ambition led to diverse assignments in advertising, graphic design and television production.

Acne witnessed a space in the market for denim and utilized this forward thinking nature to create 100 pairs of unisex jeans. The denim garnered press and short thereafter leading boutiques wanted to carry the characteristic jeans with bright-red stitching. These are the foundations of Acne.

www.acnestudios.com

ALL(ZONE)
THAILAND

Based in Bangkok, All(zone) is a group of design professionals who joyfully collaborate with specialists across the borders of their fields and country. We are fascinated by our ever-changing mega metropolis that gives a form to our everyday life. Our observations are always captured by contemporary vernacular design solutions. We, therefore, try to learn from them in order to create alternative built environments where all could feel 'at home' in the world.

www.allzonedesignall.com

ARCGENCY
DENMARK

Architectural office situated in Copenhagen, Denmark.

In the making of architecture, a high percentage of the world's resources are used. As architects, it is our responsibility to create a better world, with better cities without exploiting nature. At Arcgency we design and build sustainable architecture by using new building methods and always thinking of life-cycle and reusability. We have a strong belief, that better design last longer and creates less waste.

www.arcgency.com

AVENUE A
GERMANY

Based on 4 steps: analyze, categorize, devise, minimize; everything we conceive is designed as an object or part of an object in a comprehensive three-dimensional context. Architecture's determination is to create a sophisticated atmosphere specific to the unique user or group and urban situation. Light is one of the most important modules and inserted to guide the emotional sense through a created volume. Our work is essentially conducted by the awareness that freedom of creativity causes tremendous liability.

www.avenue-a.org

///BYN
SPAIN

///byn was founded in 2001 in Barcelona by the architects Bittor SANCHEZ-MONASTERIO and Nicolas SALTO DEL GIORGIO.

///byn is an investigative architectural office, where the interest in new conceptual research, academics, and technology based design, is applied to projects of every scale, including master plan, urban design, architecture or interior design.

www.bynstudio.com

CAROLA VANNINI ARCHITECTURE
ITALY

Carola Vannini was born in Rome in 1973; she graduated with a degree in Architecture from Rome "La Sapienza". She continued her practical education by working in the architecture and design industry in other major international cities including New York and Paris.

After two years in New York Carola returned to Rome and started her own design company, Carola Vannini Architecture, which also focuses on interior design.

Carola's approach to design stems from her diverse international experiences and respect for the use of existing contemporary architectural languages. Her design strikes a balance between the best of old and new.

Her projects are always approached with a careful eye to the clients' esthetic and functional needs, involving them in the entire creative process, up to the furniture and detailed design. This creates unique, coherent and personalized architectures.

www.carolavannini.com

CHECKLAND KINDLEYSIDES
UK

Checkland Kindleysides is an international design consultancy, renowned for our pioneering and inventive approach to brand communications and retail design.

We bring together a collaborative mix of talents and skills to create compelling, category leading brand experiences in a wide range of global and local markets.

We work with some of the most recognized and respected brands, including Sony Computer Entertainment, Wrangler, New Look, Virgin Atlantic, Umbro, ASDA and Interface.

www.checklandkindleysides.com

CHIKARA OHNO/SINATO
JAPAN

Born in Osaka 1976, Chikara Ohno studied Urban Design at Kanazawa University. After Graduation, he worked freelance and founded Sinato in 2004. Specializing in the design of private houses and commercial space as well as projects related to advertising media and art, his activities have received many awards both inside and outside of Japan. He has been serving as a part-time lecturer at Kyoto University of Art and Design since 2011.

www.sinato.jp

CHRISTIAN HALLERÖD DESIGN
SWEDEN

Johan Lytz (1974) and Christian Halleröd (1974) are working together in Stockholm. The collaboration started in 1996, and has continued in a constant dialogue concerning craftsmanship, choice of material and working methods within architecture and design. Projects at the moment are, for instance, Byredo, Acne and a villa in the Stockholm archipelago.

www.chd.se

CIGUË
FRANCE

Six architects and friends founded Ciguë in 2003 with a common passion for finding the authenticity in things, materials, spaces, and situations.

Ciguë designs and builds as one continuous process, from concept through prototypes to finished production, going back and forth from the desk to the workshop.

The company is structured around two interlinked platforms: Ciguë SARL d'architecture and Ciguë SARL de menuiserie (production unit) and a dozen of collaborators, subcontractors and artisans.

Ciguë works are diverse and different in scale: furniture, hardware, showrooms, shops, offices, restaurants, private houses, art projects, etc.

www.cigue.net

COORDINATION ASIA
CHINA

COORDINATION ASIA is founded and managed by German architect Tilman Thürmer, who also co-founded COORDINATION Berlin together with architect Jochen Gringmuth and product designer Flip Sellin. The client base of the COORDINATION studios involves global brands such as Nike, AISIDI, Falke, Adidas, Burlington, Braun and Deutsche Bank.

From cultural to commercial projects, COORDINATION ASIA's vision is that content precedes aesthetics and that great design is more than simply styling. The office is known and appreciated for this content-driven approach, as well as for a dedicated, reliable and high-standard way of working. This has resulted in successful collaborations with amongst others the Shanghai Museum of Glass and the Shanghai Film Museum.

www.coordination-asia.com

CUTIOSITY
JAPAN

Gwenael Nicolas was born in 1966 in France. After his study in RCA, London, he moved to Tokyo and established his studio "Curiosity" dealing with product, interior design and architecture. The recognizable characteristics of his designs are translucency, emotional coloring and attractive forms. If you use his products or encounter his spaces, you quickly realize that his designs are not simply about obvious beauty but that considerable thought has also gone into their functionality. The designs originate from a story-board with subjects as central focus to which he always incorporates an element of discovery and unpredictability.

curiosity.jp

DANIEL BALO
HUNGARY

Daniel Balo, Zsofi Dobos, Dora Medveczky, Judit Emese Konopas, Noemi Varga, architecture students, designed the Nanushka Beta Store in Hungary.

DESIGN OFFICE DRESS INC.
JAPAN

Design office Dress Inc, are the design studio based in Japan, working for creative which include interior, graphic and web design. "Creating the awesome experience for customers by design" is our goal.

d-dress.net

EMMANUELLE MOUREAUX
JAPAN

French architect and designer residing in Tokyo since 1996. She established "Emmanuelle Moureaux Architecture + Design" in 2003. Inspired by the Japanese traditional sliding screens, Emmanuelle has created the concept of "Shikiri", which literally means "diving (creating) space with colors" in English. She uses colors as three-dimensional elements, like layers, in order to create spaces, and not as a finishing touch applied on surfaces. Architecture, interior, furniture, products, she designs a wide range of projects, by using her unique technique of color scheming and handling color as space makers. Emmanuelle Moureaux is an Associate professor at the Tohoko University of Art & Design, member of the "Tokyo society of architects", "Architectural Institute of Japan", "Japan Institute of Architects".

www.emmanuelle.jp

FABIO NOVEMBRE
ITALY

Since 1966, I've responded to those who call me Fabio Novembre.

Since 1992, I've responded to those who also call me "architect".

I cut out spaces in the vacuum by blowing air bubbles, and I make gifts of sharpened pins so as to insure I never put on airs.

My lungs are imbued with the scent of places that I've breathed, and when I hyperventilate it's only so I can remain in apnea for a while.

As though I were pollen, I let myself go with the wind, convinced I'm able to seduce everything that surrounds me.

I want to breathe till I choke.
I want to love till I die.

www.novembre.it

FORM US WITH LOVE
SWEDEN

FORM US WITH LOVE is a design studio operating from Stockholm. The studio was started in 2005 and has since pushed to challenge the conventional through design initiatives. FUWL partners with companies involved in the development and production of everyday objects, furniture and lighting. Clients include Scandinavian and international brands such as ateljé Lyktan, Bolon, Cappellini, DePadova, Muuto, Design House Sthlm and One Nordic Furniture Company.

In 2012 Form Us With Love was named by Fast Company as one of the world's 50 most influential designers shaping the future. In 2013 Form Us With Love was awarded "designer of the year" by ELLE Decoration Sweden.

www.formuswithlove.se

GREG NATALE DESIGN
AUSTRALIA

Since 2001, Greg Natale Design has been pioneering the integration of design and decoration; focusing on residential, retail and commercial design. With a bold signature style, Greg Natale Design is instantly recognized alongside Australia's top designers. Greg Natale Design has won numerous awards, appeared in local and international press including Wallpaper, British Elle and has been published in many design books flanking renowned international designers. At the 2011 Belle Coco Republic Interior Design Awards Greg won the award for Interior Designer of the Year.

Greg Natale Design offers a full design service for its clients from concept design, documentation and council approvals, through to construction administration, as well as interior decoration.

gregnatale.com

HOTEL CREATIVE
UK

We are a multi-disciplined creative consultancy based in soho specializing in concepts, design and art direction, our services also extend to branding, identity, exhibitions and events.

We pride ourselves on our ability to understand and deliver great ideas along with high quality production, attention to detail and a high standard of installation.

www.hotelcreative.co.uk

IÑIGO BEGUIRISTAIN + IÑAKI BERGERA
SPAIN

Iñigo Beguiristain received his Diploma in Architecture (1998) from the University of Navarre in Pamplona, Spain. He teaches as Associated Professor at the University of the Basque Country. Iñaki Bergera received his Diploma in Architecture (1997) and PhD. (2002) from the University of Navarre and he currently teaches as Design Professor at the University of Saragossa. They both have been visiting teachers, guest critics or lecturers at several international universities. They have received several awards in architectural design competitions. Widely published in design magazines, their work on the field of interior design has received many awards.

www.ibeguiristain.com

KEISUKE FUJIWARA
JAPAN

Keisuke Fujiwara was born in 1968 in Tokyo, Japan. He graduated the Musashino Art University, and followed to work under the renowned interior designer, Shigeru Uchida. After interning at Ron Arad Associates in 2001, he established Keisuke Fujiwara Design Office which specializes in interior and furniture design. He has been designing shops for PLEATS PLEASE ISSEY MIYAKE around the world (Japan, France, China, South Korea, Taiwan and Thailand). Since establishing Keisuke Fujiwara Design Office, his work has been exhibited in the Milan furniture fair, DESIGN MIAMI and INTERIEUR in Kortrijk. He was awarded first prize from the Japanese Commercial Environment Designer Association. He currently holds an Associate Professor position at the Tokyo Metropolitan University.

www.keisukefujiwara.com

KINZO
GERMANY

The Berlin-based office KINZO was founded in 1998. Starting from interior projects for shops, lofts and offices, fairs and exhibitions as well as design for events and film sets, the three architects and founders of the company Karim El-Ishmawi, Chris Middleton and Martin Jacobs have become famous for their distinctive, sport and science-fiction inspired elegance. In 2008, KINZO successfully ventured into product design: Its office furniture programme KINZO AIR was awarded the red dot design award and nominated for the 2009 German State Design Price. The following years the designers focus on their most distinctive project so far: The office space and furniture program for adidas new headquarter, making the gigantic office complex a dazzling experience.

www.kinzo-berlin.de

KOIS ARCHITECTURE
GREECE

Kois Associated Architects is based in Athens and was founded by architect Stelios Kois in 2007. K.A.A work encompasses all fields of design, ranging from urban projects to private buildings, interiors, furniture and products. The design ethos of the collaboration is the synchronized engagement in practice and research that leads to the evaluation and generation of new solutions. Research topics are drawn from natural formal and social sciences in an attempt to form an interdisciplinary network of information that will inform the decision making process. We work in a continuous workshop spirit with a multidisciplinary team of architects, engineers, graphic artists and town planners from different cultural backgrounds. The practice's view is that only through diversity and antithesis true innovative solution emerges and manifests its self.

www.koisarchitecture.com

LUIGI VALENTE ARCHITECTURE
ITALY

Architecture, design, art and photography. Today, there is no creativity without the ability of mixing styles, languages and Medias Starting from this belief, the firm has chosen to act on a multi-sector level, while deeply exploring the different aspect of Design. Research and substantiality are the main aspects of our work, whose main purpose is to find a balance between drawing and realization, concept design and field-work. Fully embroiled into the international debate, the firm is deeply looking into new sustainable building techniques, while applying them to different aspects of architectural work, with main attention to restoration and refurbishment projects. A dynamic, open and young professional approach is applied to the way of conceiving the Architecture, both to its present and past, looking forward an upcoming future, that still is waiting to be designed.

www.luigivalente.com

MOMENT INC.
JAPAN

Hisaaki Hirawata and Tomohiro Watabe established MOMENT Inc. in 2005.

The projects are wide-ranging as graphic, product, interior, and architecture.

Hirawata and Watabe attempt to suggest strong design-message which is not compressed in a category. 2D and 3D is an equal theme to every kinds of design project.

www.moment-design.com

NORIYUKI OTSUKA
JAPAN

Born in Fukui Japan, 1960. Otsuka travelled to Europe after graduating from design school in Tokyo. He worked as interior designer at Plastic Studio and Associates after returning to Japan. In 1990, he founded Noriyuki Otsuka Design Office Inc.

His design policy "Nothing is everything / Mixtures of transparency" are reflected in his works for boutiques, restaurants, private residences, furniture and product designs.

In 2003, he participated in Milano Fuori Salone in cooperation with the STRATO Co. (Italian kitchen company).

www.nodo.jp

PHANOS KYRIACOU
GERMANY

Phanos Kyriacou studied at Middlesex School of Fine Arts and Goldsmith's University, London. He lives and works in Nicosia and Berlin. In 2003 Kyriacou created 'Midget Factory' an artist running space in the old part of the town of Nicosia, from where he carried out various projects that create a dialogue between art and the urban landscape.

Since 2002has presented work in many solo and group exhibitions in Cyprus and abroad Among the more recent are: Terra Mediterranea – In Crisis, NiMAC/Mapping Cyprus: Contemporary Views, Bozar, Brussels / XO, Grim museum, Berlin / Spending dark days in the sun, Kinderhook&Caracas, Berlin / Utopia: New acquisitions from the collection of Nicos Chr. Pattichis, Evagoras Lanitis Center, Limassol/ Everyone should walk, Salon Populaire, Berlin.

www.phanoskyriacou.com

PLAJER & FRANZ STUDIO
GERMANY

Plajer & Franz Studio is an international and interdisciplinary team of 45 architects, interior architects and graphic designers based in berlin. All project stages – from concept to design as well as roll-out supervision – are carried out in-house. Special project-based teams work on over all interior and building construction projects and on communication and graphic design.

www.plajer-franz.de

PROCESS5 DESIGN
JAPAN

Process5 Degisn was started as Process5 by Noriaki Takeda and Ikuma Yoshizawa in 1999. The office was established as Process5 Design in 2009 in Osaka Japan. PROCESS5 DESIGN designs architecture, interior, and graphic which valued the concept regardless of use.

Noriaki Takeda was born in Osaka in 1980. He received his degree from the architectural course of Kinki University in 2003. After worked for MARIO DELMARE (2003-2006), he established office.

Ikuma Yoshizawa was born in Nara in 1980. He received his degree from the architectural course of Kinki University in 2003. After worked for AMORPHE Takeyama & Associates (2003-2009), he established office.

process5.com

PT GREEN DESIGN
INDONESIA

PT Green Design is located in Indonesia, belong to Indonesian owner. The studio lead by Giovanni D'Ambrosio has been working in architecture and industrial design fields for several years. The studio considers project creativity as the heart of the design that is the result of an interaction with the customer, an interaction which leads to share project opinions. The work philosophy is based on the relationship between architecture and nature and consequently between outdoor and indoor spaces. Our studio built an international reputation especially with projects in Europe, Australia, and Indonesia. International publications and contemporary critics support our activity.

www.ptgreenhome.com

RDAI
FRANCE

RDAI is imbued with the rigor and elegance of its founder, Rena Dumas. Her legacy of excellence, exactingness and ethics are the forces that guide Denis Montel towards the future of the agency that he directs today, after 10 years of close collaboration with her. Since its inception in 1972, RDAI has transcended the boundaries between architecture, interior architecture and design. Today, Denis Montel and his team deepen this commitment and carry forward the development of an international agency.

Each project is approached with an understanding of the contexts and situations that stimulate the imagination and justify taking a particular standpoint. Without any preconceived ideas on its dimension, whether it's an interior space, a building or an object, RDAI proposes a project-environment that is one and indivisible. RDAI claims that architecture is the reflection of the epoch we live in.

www.rdai.fr

REIICHI IKEDA
JAPAN

In 1981, Reiichi Ikeda was born in Shiga prefecture, Japan. In 2011, he established REIICHI IKEDA DESIGN.

His wide-ranging design works are from renovation plans for housings and condominium buildings to shop interiors including restaurants, beauty salons, clothing boutiques, wedding facilities, and so on.

The striking feature of his design is not only a decorative value, but also the logical concept derived from the accumulation of every situation and information.

reiichiikeda.com

RIFE DESIGNS
SOUTH AFRICA

Client's require excellent design and fast turnaround times. Rife is a streamlined operation that meets those needs. Over 20 years combined experience has given us an excellent understanding of our client's business and their requirements. To complement our excellent internal resources we have a pool of talented freelancers that offer top quality design in their various areas of expertise. They give us the man power as and when we need it to deliver on time. Working closely with our creative director freelancers brings new and fresh ideas to the table. New ideas are always welcome in the design business. We've eliminated the red tape and bureaucratic systems that stifle creativity, waste time and compromise deadlines.

www.rifedesigns.co.za

ROBIN SLUIJZER
THE NETHERLANDS

Robin Sluijzer is known as a leading designer. He develops interior concepts for exclusive apartments, houses, fashion stores, restaurants, clubs and hotels. Founded by Robin Sluijzer in 1999 the studio is based in the heart of Amsterdam. Together with a team of professionals and partners the Studio is involved in the entire project, from design to completion.

Studio Robin Sluijzer realizes projects internationally appreciated by quality and a distinctive identity.

www.robinsluijzer.com

S1 ARCHITEKTUR
GERMANY

S1 Architektur is an architectural studio based in Berlin, Germany.

It's managed by architects Henning Ziepke and Ansgar Schmidt.

www.s1architektur.com

SAQ
BELGIUM

SAQ is a conceptual and interdisciplinary design agency specialized in developing spatial sceneries and concepts.

The practice relies on a broad range of competencies where architects, interior designers, urbanists, video-artists and graphic designers team up according to the specific orientation or necessities of each project. SAQ believes strongly in co-operation and regularly invites professional experts or companies to participate in the materialization or the elaboration of an idea. For SAQ scale is no parameter. Intensive research, sketching, simulation, and dialogue are the fundaments of an intensive creative process leading to proposals for both small scaled designs and macro-planning.

saq.eu

SERRANO + BAQUERO

SPAIN

Juan Antonio Serrano Garcia and Paloma Baquero Masats are architects, graduated in the School of Architecture of Granada in 2009. They have a PhD in Advanced Architectural Design (School of Architecture of Madrid).

The office Serrano + Baquero was constituted in 2010, making urban, interiorism and architecture projects. The more outstanding ones may be 'Rurban Geology' and 'NewWaterGarden', that resulted winning projects in Europan XI contest (2011), and horizontal showcase, a little store built in Granada in 2010.

At the moment, both architects are focusing on investigation, conducting several investigation projects on urban issues and working on their doctoral thesis, and assisting as teachers in the School of Architecture of Madrid.

www.serranoybaquero.com

SIGURD LARSEN DESIGN & ARCHITECTURE

GERMANY

Sigurd Larsen is a Berlin based Danish architect working within the fields of design, art and architecture. He has a master degree from The Royal Academy of Fine Arts, School of Architecture in Copenhagen and previously been employed at OMA-Rem Koolhaas in New York, MVRDV in Rotterdam, Cobe Architects in Copenhagen and Topotek1 in Berlin.

Sigurd Larsen founded the design studio in 2009 and has recently realized projects for Voo Store in Berlin, K-MB Agentur für Markenkommunikation GmbH and Zalando Labels. His furniture have been exhibited at fairs and galleries in Berlin, Helsinki, Hong Kong, Tokyo, Seoul and Shanghai. The work of the design studio combines the aesthetics of high quality materials with concepts focusing on functionality in complex spaces.

www.sigurdlarsen.eu

SOME

FRANCE

Some is a young Paris based architecture firm founded by Rémi Souleau and Benoît Meriac.

For SOME, each project is a way to ask about the way we live, future of our social condition or contemporary construction. Each project is a condition to ask questions, to run on defaults and finally to reveal invisible problems by a project which is more than a simple draw. SOME needs to "DO WITH" and not to "DENY IT". Being inspired by this "ALREADY THERE" is the basement of their Architecture. Maybe because of their formation, SOME is very careful about societal reflexion, technical and green solutions, every time for one goal: giving an Ambitious, Attentive and Adequate Architecture for everybody. That's the founder's aim to give the most respectful solution in a society which is ever and ever in movement. From the emergence of an idea to its realisation, SOME has developed "un savoir faire" and a very specifically methodology, that they shape better and better every day.

www.some-architecture.com

SPECIALNORMAL INC.

JAPAN

Specialnormal Inc. is a multidisciplinary design office based in the heart of Tokyo. It was founded by Shin Takahashi in 2011, and within a year it already built a great portfolio such as Note et Silence, Quiksilver Store Toyosu and Baccarat 2011 S/S Collection.

Shin Takahashi is a founder and principal designer of Specialnormal Inc.

He studied an interior design at Kuwasawa Design Institute. Prior to founding Specialnormal Inc., he was engaged in several projects with world-class retail brands.

special-normal.com

STONE DESIGNS

SPAIN

Stone Designs is the story of two creators (Cutu Mazuelos 1973 and Eva Prego 1974) who in September 1995 started their adventure by creating their own studio, in order to develop their projects from a personal perspective, without censureship or interference. This allows them to concentrate exclusively on what they do best, designing. It has left them time to take on projects of much greater depth and to work with companies with which they truly feel an affinity with. Being independant has its advantages...It is the story of two young hopefuls desiring to tell things in a different way. It is the constant search for new languages, a journey to the heart of the people around them doing what they do best – design? No! But telling real stories, from within, sincerely full of experiences, of problems and later on, joy. In this sincere way, they show whenever they create something or give a conference, that they do it with naturalness and energy, with unusual excitement, despite their experience.

www.stone-dsgns.com

TAO THONG VILLA

JAPAN

Tao Thong Villa was established by Hideki Kureha in April 1996.

He does wide range of work, wedding photography, commercial photography, graphic design, interior design as well as architectural work. His main office is located in Aoyama, Tokyo; brunches are in Nagano, Matsumoto, Osaka, and Himeji.

www.taothongvilla.co.jp

WUDAI SHIGUO

CHINA

Wudai Shiguo is a state-of-the-art creative boutique based in Hong Kong, specialized in creative design, branding consultancy, visual communication and always keep reaching for new forms of expression. Powered by a crew of rebels, the young establishment has been tipped.

www.wudai-shiguo.com